PEARSON

Glenview, Illinois
Boston, Massachusetts
Chandler, Arizona
Upper Saddle River, New Jersey

Copyright © 2014 Pearson Education, Inc., or its affiliates. All Rights Reserved. Printed in the United States of America. This publication is protected by copyright, and permission should be obtained from the publisher prior to any prohibited reproduction, storage in a retrieval system, or transmission in any form or by any means, electronic, mechanical, photocopying, recording, or likewise. For information regarding permissions, write to Rights Management & Contracts, One Lake Street, Upper Saddle River, New Jersey 07458.

ReadyGEN is a trademark, in the U.S. and/or other countries, of Pearson Education, Inc., or its affiliates.

Common Core State Standards: © Copyright 2010. National Governors Association Center for Best Practices and Council of Chief State School Officers. All rights reserved.

ISBN-13: 978-0-328-78989-4
ISBN-10:   0-328-78989-5
2 3 4 5 6 7 8 9 10 V056 17 16 15 14 13

Contents

Super Sleuth Steps 4

Unit 1 Understanding Communities 6
The Hunt for Amelia's Ring 8
A Birthday Surprise 10
Unlikely Friends 12

Unit 2 Making Decisions 14
I'll Trade You! 16
More Than Cash Dispensers 18
Another Movie Night to Remember 20

Unit 3 Building Ideas 22
Gregor Mendel 24
A Few Good Words 26
Josh Gibson, Home Run King 28

Unit 4 Facing Challenges and Change 30
A Real-Life Action Hero 32
The Blank Book 34
Curtis the Cowboy Cook 36

Unit 5 Pioneering New Ideas and New Worlds 38
Journey to Freedom 40
A Journey North 42
From Seed to Flower to Fruit 44

Unit 6 Changing the World 46
Picking Up Sunset Park 48
Making a Difference, One Bag at a Time 50
Wanted: Great Student Leaders! 52

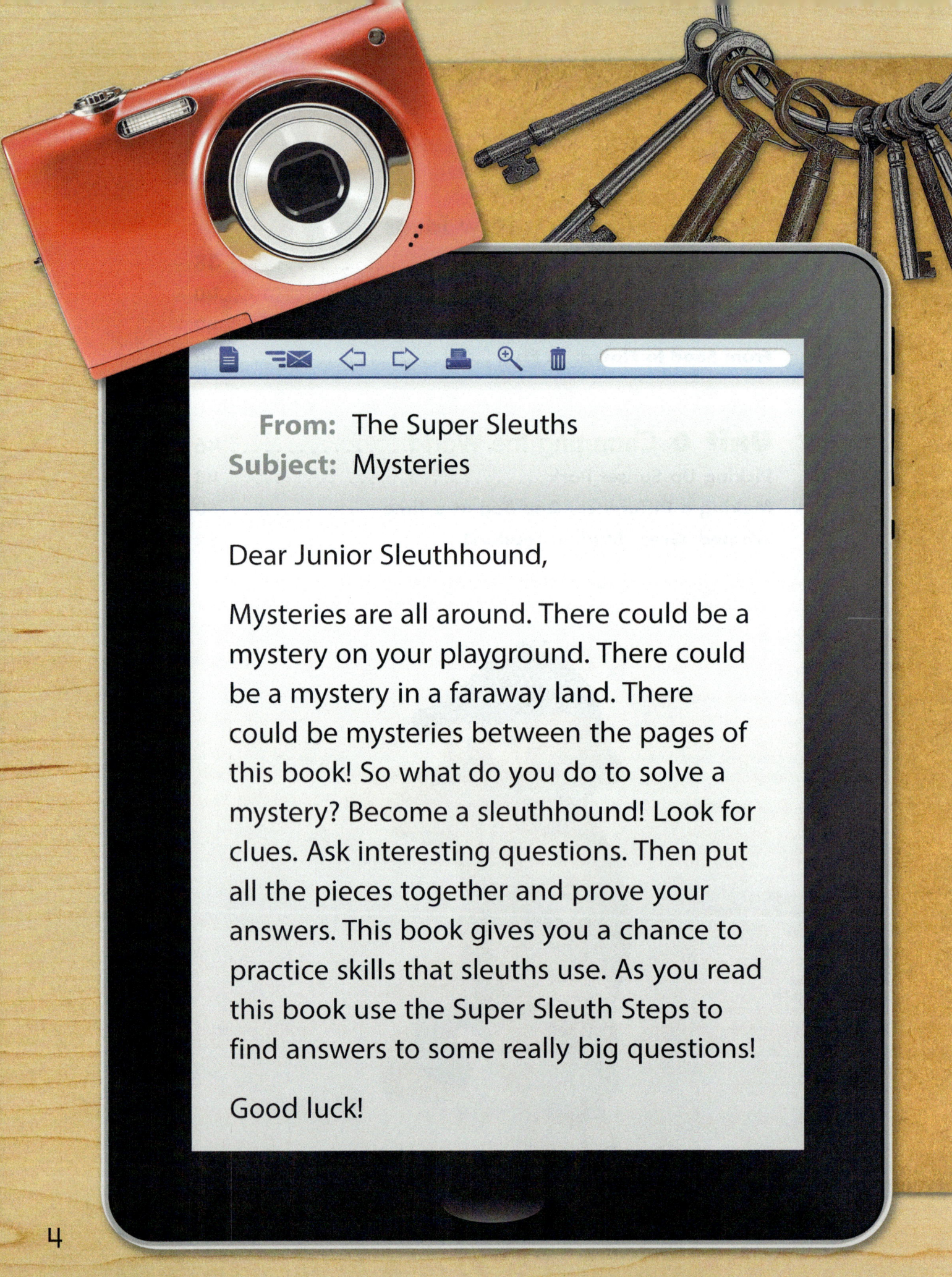

From: The Super Sleuths
Subject: Mysteries

Dear Junior Sleuthhound,

Mysteries are all around. There could be a mystery on your playground. There could be a mystery in a faraway land. There could be mysteries between the pages of this book! So what do you do to solve a mystery? Become a sleuthhound! Look for clues. Ask interesting questions. Then put all the pieces together and prove your answers. This book gives you a chance to practice skills that sleuths use. As you read this book use the Super Sleuth Steps to find answers to some really big questions!

Good luck!

SUPER SLEUTH STEPS

Look for Clues
- Look back through the text and pictures. What do they tell you?
- Write or draw what you learn. It will help you remember.
- Look for important ideas and try to put the clues together.

Ask Questions
- Super sleuths ask great questions.
- Be curious.
- Try to find out more.

Make Your Case
- Look at all the clues and summarize what you know.
- Use what you learn and already know to think of your own ideas.
- Tell what you think.

Prove It!
- Show what you have learned.
- Work with others. Share the adventure!

Unit 1
Understanding Communities

Hi, Sleuthhounds! In this unit, you will be looking for clues as we explore how people live and work together. Here are some sleuth tips to help you. Enjoy the adventure!

Sleuth Tips

Look for Clues
Where do sleuths find clues?
- Sleuths look at the words. Some clues may be hidden.
- Sleuths find clues in the pictures. Look closely.

Ask Questions
What kinds of questions do sleuths ask?
- Sleuths ask what happened.
- Sleuths try to learn when, where, why, and how something happened.

Make Your Case
How do sleuths decide on an answer?
- Sleuths look back at what they read. They think about what they already know.
- Sleuths look at the clues. Clues may point to the best answer.

Prove It!
What do sleuths do to prove what they know?
- Sleuths think about all they have learned and decide what is important to share.
- Sleuths plan what they will share and check their work.

The Hunt for Amelia's Ring

"Janine, have you seen my ring?" Amelia asked.

Janine *had* seen her sister's ring. She had tried it on, but it was a little big, so she took it off . . . but where did she put it? Janine couldn't remember!

When she told her sister the truth, Amelia was upset. Janine had to find that ring! She crawled under tables, peeked inside dresser drawers, looked behind the couch, and opened every cabinet. Finally, she gave up and went outside to sit on the front steps.

Her neighbor, Mrs. Kim, came up the stairs. "What's wrong?" she asked. Janine told her.

"I find it is useful to retrace my steps when I can't find something," Mrs. Kim said.

Janine thought and thought. First, she had done homework, and then she had a snack. Then . . . ah, ha! She remembered!

Janine helped carry Mrs. Kim's groceries. Then she ran to her apartment and went to the kitchen windowsill. There it was! The ring was right where Janine had left it when she helped water Mom's plants. Janine ran to give it to Amelia. She had learned her lesson about taking what wasn't hers. She also learned that two heads are better than one when there is a mystery to solve!

Be a Sleuth

Look for Clues How did Mrs. Kim's suggestion help Janine find the ring? Look for clues in the text.

Ask Questions After reading this text, what questions would you have asked Janine to help her find the ring?

Make Your Case How do you think the relationship between Janine and her sister change from the beginning of the story to the end? Explain your thinking.

A Birthday Surprise

"Mom will be so surprised!" Sadie said. She looked proudly at the cake that Uncle Curt had helped her and her brother Sam make for Mom's birthday.

"Let's put it in the dining room," Sam said. "That way it will be the first thing Mom sees."

Sadie agreed, and Sam carefully picked it up. Then trouble arrived. Their cousin Wes bounded through the swinging door. The door bumped the plate, the plate tipped, and *splat!* The cake landed on the floor.

"Oh, no!" Sadie cried. "What can we do now?"

"We'll have to be creative," Sam said.

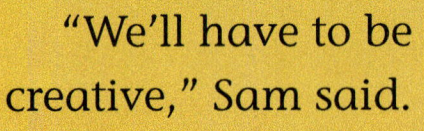

Uncle Curt had made them pancakes that morning before he left for work, and they still had leftovers. "We can't give Mom a birthday cake. Let's give her birthday pancakes instead!" Sadie said.

"Great idea!" said Sam. They warmed the pancakes. Sam spread jam on each one. Then Sadie put on banana slices. They stacked the pancakes and put candles on top.

Just then, they heard Mom coming down the stairs. Sam raced to the stairs and asked her to stay in her bedroom. Mom thought there might be a surprise. Then Sadie arrived with the birthday pancakes. Mom laughed. "How did you know that I have always wanted to have a birthday breakfast in bed?" she said.

Be a Sleuth

Look for Clues What clues tell you about Sadie's talents and personality?

Ask Questions What questions would you have asked if you had been there when the cake fell?

Make Your Case Why is sequence important in this story? Use examples from the story in your answer.

Unlikely Friends

Every Monday afternoon, Anya helped Ms. Hickson with her yard work. Ms. Hickson always watched Anya from her tall porch. She even had a glass of juice waiting for her when the work was done. Anya often brought along her violin. Ms. Hickson would beam with delight when Anya played for her. Anya used to complain about visiting Ms. Hickson, but Anya's mother always insisted she go. She said that neighbors should take care of each other.

One Monday, Anya came without her violin. When she finished raking the yard, she sat down sadly beside her neighbor. Ms. Hickson asked what had happened. Anya burst into tears. Her brother had broken her violin by accident. There was no way it could be fixed in time for her fall concert.

Ms. Hickson disappeared into the house. She returned a few minutes later with an old violin case.

Inside was the most beautiful violin Anya had ever seen. Ms. Hickson picked it up lovingly and handed it to Anya. Anya played a few notes, laid the violin in its velvet-lined case, and threw her arms around Ms. Hickson. The violin was the best gift Anya had ever received.

Be a Sleuth

Look for Clues Find clues that show Anya and Ms. Hickson were good neighbors.

Ask Questions What questions would you ask Ms. Hickson if you were visiting her?

Make Your Case What do we know about the relationship between Anya and Ms. Hickson? Use detail from the story in your answer.

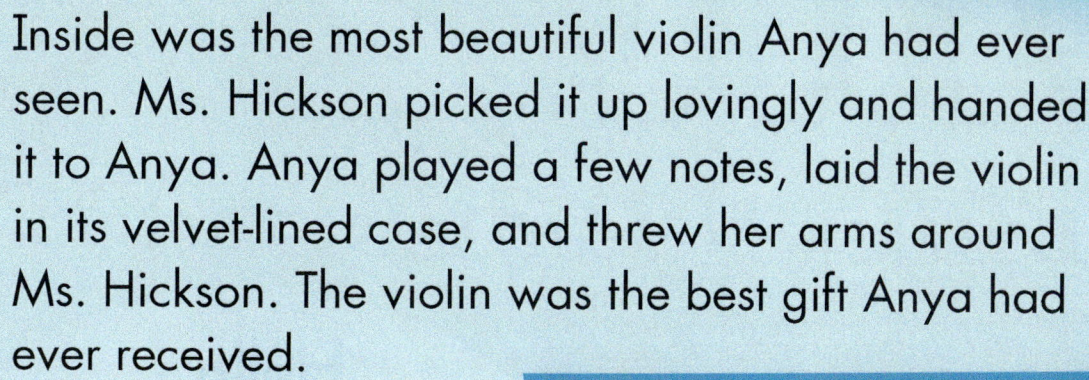

Unit 2
Making Decisions

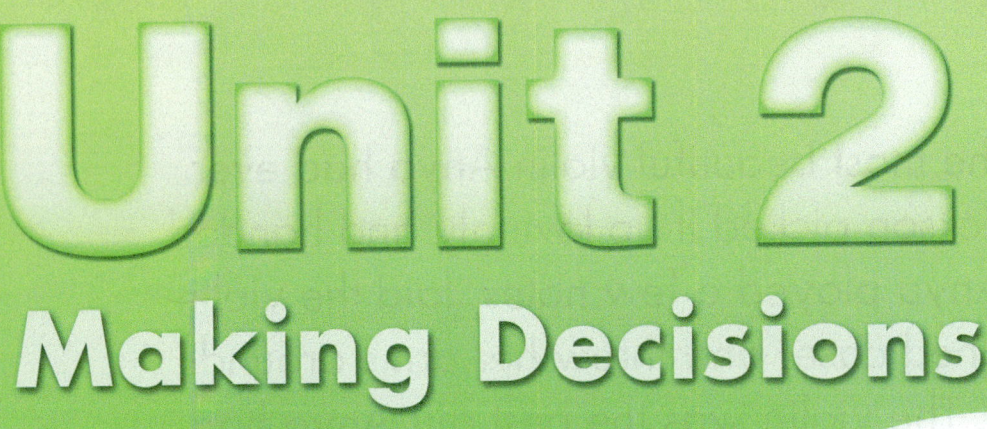

Hello, Sleuthhounds! In this unit, you will be looking for clues to learn how people make decisions. Here are some sleuth tips to help you. Good luck!

Sleuth Tips

Look for Clues

Why do sleuths reread?
- Sleuths reread because they know they may miss something the first time.
- Sleuths reread to find hidden clues!

Ask Questions

What makes a great question?
- Sleuths know that a great question is focused on the topic.
- Sleuths choose their words carefully when they ask a question.

Make Your Case

How do sleuths make a clear case?
- Sleuths clearly state what they believe at the beginning and again at the end.
- Sleuths tell the clues they found in the text and pictures.

Prove It!

What do sleuths do when they work with other sleuths?
- Sleuths share what they know. This is the time to share your clues with others.
- Sleuths share the work so everyone gets a chance to shine!

I'll Trade You!

Samuel couldn't wait to show his mom and grandma the new skateboard he had just gotten from Ben. Ben couldn't wait to give his sister the new shawl he had just gotten from Samuel. Ben and Samuel were best friends!

Samuel's grandma had worked for weeks knitting the shawl. Ben had wondered for weeks what to get his sister for her birthday. Then one night Ben saw the shawl Samuel's grandma was knitting. He knew his sister would love it!

Samuel spent every day after school skateboarding with Ben. Samuel wished for his own skateboard. Ben knew how much Samuel would love having a skateboard. Suddenly a trade was born!

Trading one thing for another was a way of life. Samuel's mom and grandma remembered when people used something called money instead.

Money paid for things they needed. Samuel and Ben were too young to remember that time.

   Sometimes, Samuel's mother opened a secret drawer in her jewelry box. She let him hold the shiny coins and smooth dollar bills she had saved. Then they were put away for safekeeping.

   People no longer used money. They traded things instead. Samuel couldn't imagine life any other way. Samuel knew how to draw, so he always traded his drawings to get what he wanted. His family and Ben's family traded often. Samuel didn't understand why anyone might need money. Trading was so much easier!

Sleuth Work

Gather Evidence How can you tell that this story takes place some time in the future? Write details that support this.

Ask Questions If you could talk with Samuel and Ben, what questions would you ask them about life without money? Write two questions.

Make Your Case What is the most important idea the writer wants to share about trading? What information is given to support that idea?

17

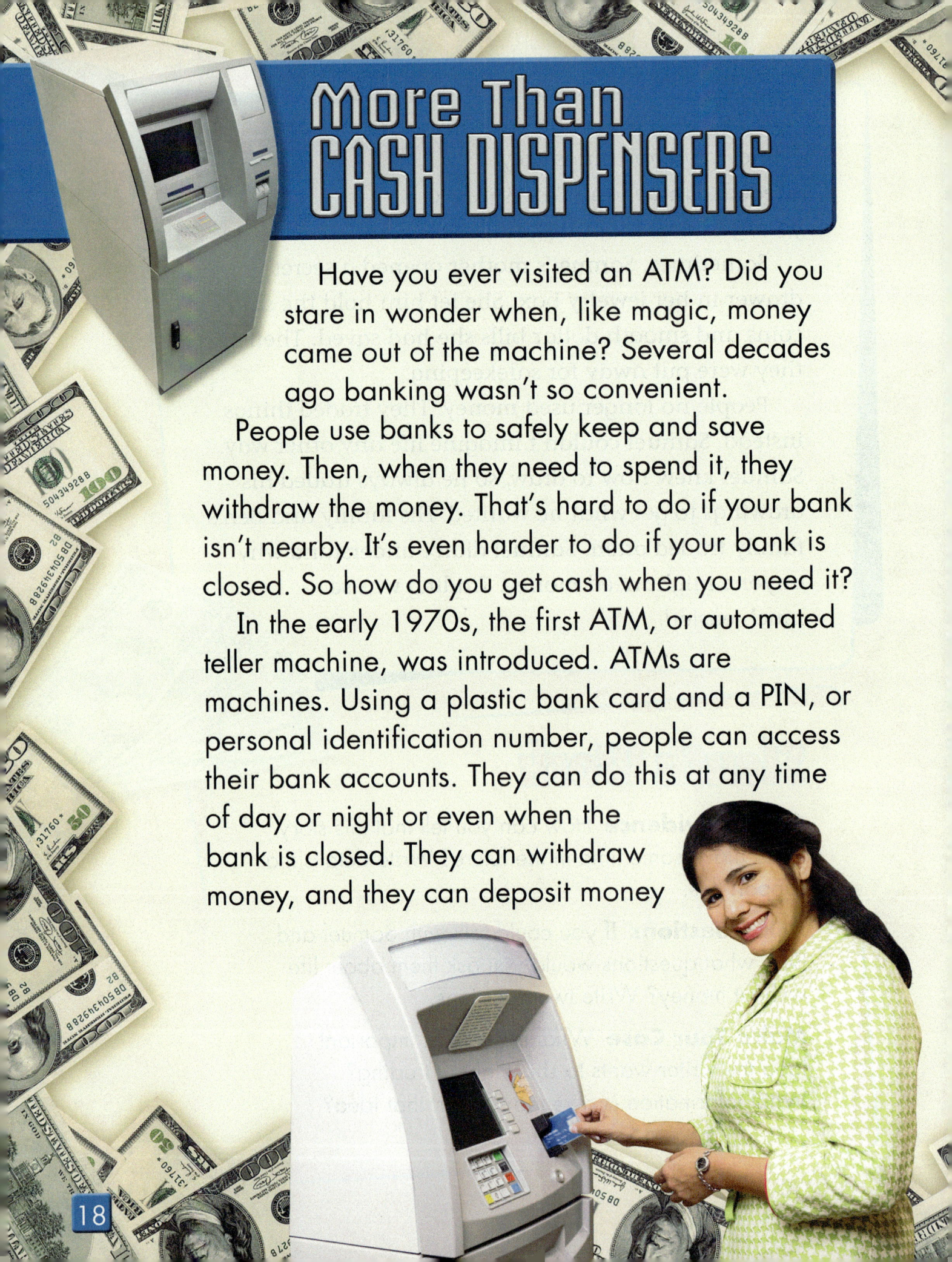

More Than CASH DISPENSERS

Have you ever visited an ATM? Did you stare in wonder when, like magic, money came out of the machine? Several decades ago banking wasn't so convenient.

People use banks to safely keep and save money. Then, when they need to spend it, they withdraw the money. That's hard to do if your bank isn't nearby. It's even harder to do if your bank is closed. So how do you get cash when you need it?

In the early 1970s, the first ATM, or automated teller machine, was introduced. ATMs are machines. Using a plastic bank card and a PIN, or personal identification number, people can access their bank accounts. They can do this at any time of day or night or even when the bank is closed. They can withdraw money, and they can deposit money and checks. What's even more helpful is that ATMs can be found everywhere!

Banks are adding new ATM services every year. For example, people can now deposit checks without using an envelope. That's because ATMs scan, or read, checks. Another improvement is talking ATMs. These machines have audio, so people who cannot see well or at all can access their bank accounts by listening to instructions.

ATMs keep improving. Some ATMs now have video screens. A banker uses the video screen to talk with the person using the ATM. Other banks are even testing ways mobile phones can be used at ATMs. Just imagine what ATMs will be able to do next!

SLEUTH WORK

Gather Evidence How are modern ATMs different from ATMs from the early 1970s? Give at least one piece of evidence from the text.

Ask Questions After reading the text, what ATM service would you like to learn more about? Write a question to guide your research.

Make Your Case What information does the writer give to support the idea that ATMs are more than cash dispensers?

Another Movie Night to Remember

For weeks, I had seen a big, red circle on the calendar. It was my parents' anniversary. I got the sense this was an important day, and I wanted to do something to celebrate . . . but what? Mom had once told us that Dad asked her to marry him after taking her out for pizza and a romantic movie. We decided to have a movie night that Mom and Dad would never forget.

We bought the ingredients to make Mom's favorite pizza. My older sister Bethany found out what movie they had seen, and we rented it for the night. But everything started to go wrong.

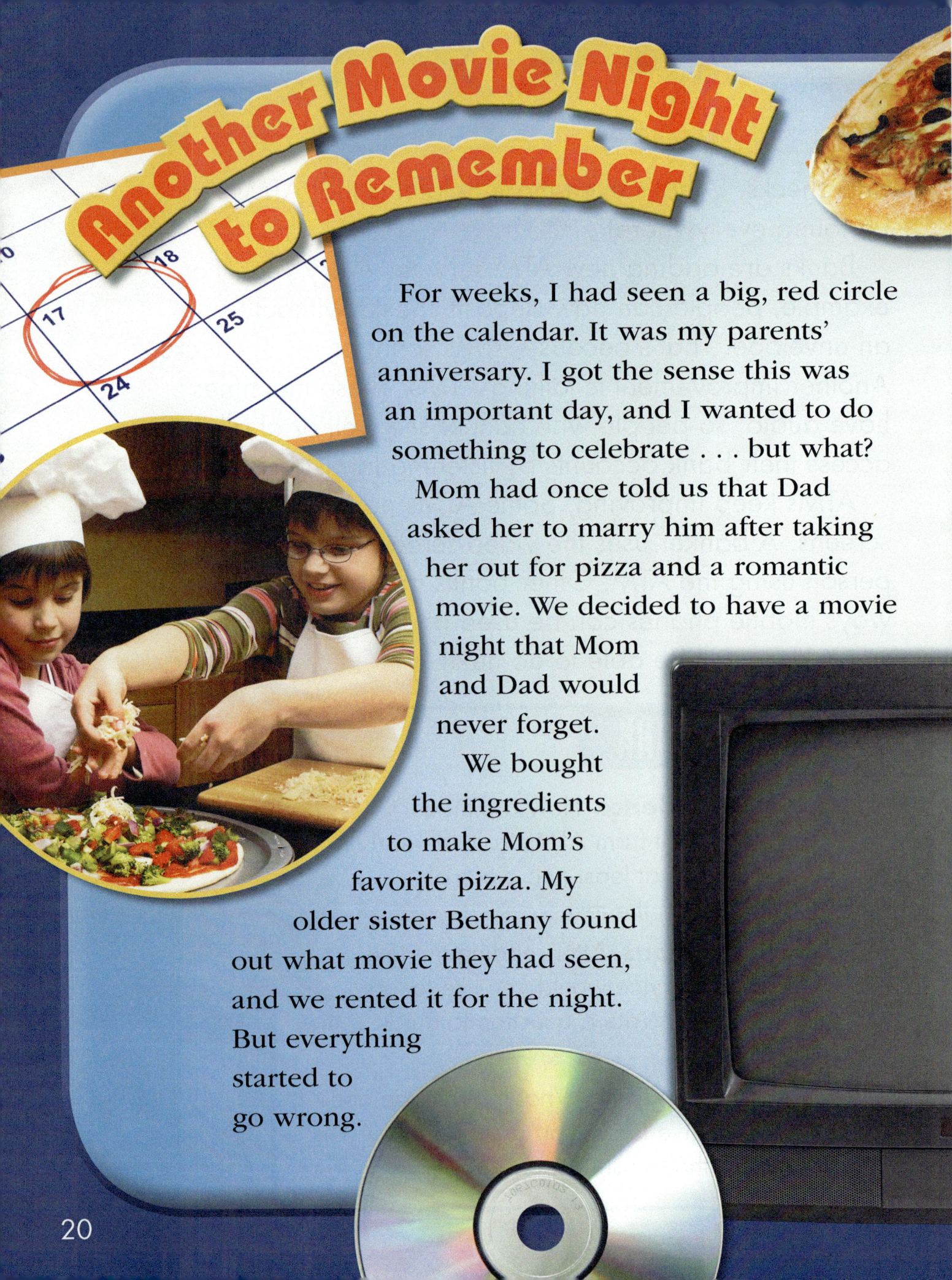

First, the pizza slid off the pan and onto the floor as I carried it to the table. Next, Bethany burned the popcorn, so the whole house smelled awful. Then we discovered that the DVD wouldn't play. Bethany and I were upset, but Dad chuckled as he opened a window to air out the house. He took us out to dinner, to the same restaurant where he and Mom had eaten that special night. Over pizza, we heard the story of how Mom and Dad met. It was better than the best romantic movie—even without popcorn!

Be a Sleuth

Look for Clues What clues can you find to show that Mom and Dad were not upset about the problems that happened with the surprise?

Ask Questions After reading the text, what questions would you ask someone who is celebrating a special day?

Make Your Case Choose words the writer used to describe her feelings. Replace them with words that have similar meanings. Read the story aloud.

Unit 3
Building Ideas

Hello there, Sleuthhounds! In this unit, you will be looking for clues about some big ideas. Here are some sleuth tips to help you. Have fun!

Sleuth Tips

Look for Clues

How do sleuths get clues from pictures?
- Sleuths use pictures to help them figure out harder words or ideas.
- Sleuths look at pictures to learn things that are not included in the text.

Ask Questions

Why are sleuths so curious?
- Sleuths always wonder why or how something happened. They try to find something others didn't notice.
- Sleuths know that being curious and asking questions can lead to adventures!

Make Your Case

Why don't all sleuths agree on the answers?
- Sleuths may find different clues or put the clues together in different ways.
- Sleuths know that our different experiences cause each of us to think differently.

Prove It!

How can sleuths be creative when showing what they have learned?
- Sleuths try to use new and different ways to show details clearly.
- Sleuths think of many ways to share what they know. They might draw, write, or put on a show!

Gregor Mendel

Gregor Mendel always loved nature. He grew up on a farm. He walked through the countryside every day. He loved to look at plants and animals along the way. He noticed the ways plants are alike and different. Later, Mendel became a teacher and scientist.

One day Mendel took a long walk. He saw a flower that was different from others of the same kind. It made him wonder. What caused such differences? He began to grow pea plants as part of an experiment. In seven years, he grew thousands of plants! He kept track of different traits in plants. He noticed the color of the flowers and pea pods. He measured the height of the plants. He noticed the shape of their pods and leaves. He saw that there was a pattern. "Parent" plants passed traits to "daughter" plants in certain ways. Mendel's studies helped him discover rules about how traits are passed on. This was the beginning of a branch of science called genetics.

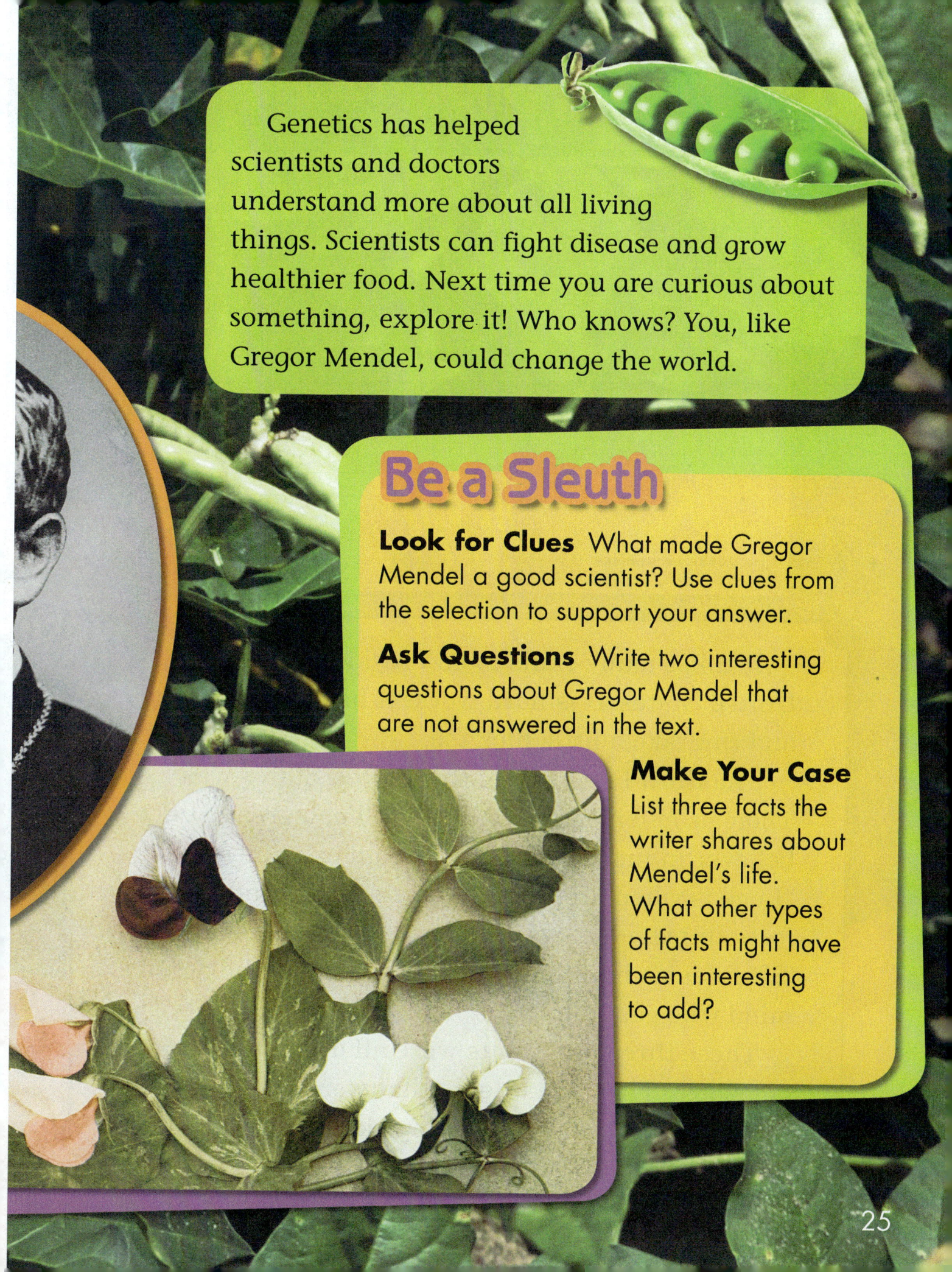

Genetics has helped scientists and doctors understand more about all living things. Scientists can fight disease and grow healthier food. Next time you are curious about something, explore it! Who knows? You, like Gregor Mendel, could change the world.

Be a Sleuth

Look for Clues What made Gregor Mendel a good scientist? Use clues from the selection to support your answer.

Ask Questions Write two interesting questions about Gregor Mendel that are not answered in the text.

Make Your Case List three facts the writer shares about Mendel's life. What other types of facts might have been interesting to add?

A Few Good Words

It takes many skills to be President of the United States. It is hard work. It has few rewards and can take a little luck too.

The third President of the United States was Thomas Jefferson. He once said, "I'm a great believer in luck." Abraham Lincoln explained that, "Luck is when preparation meets opportunity." Our fortieth president was Ronald Reagan. He said, "There is no limit to what a man can do if he doesn't mind who gets the credit."

These three presidents were all different kinds of leaders. They had talents that were special.

Thomas Jefferson had many skills and helped found our country. He was born in 1743 in Virginia.

He was an architect, musician, and scientist. He wrote the Declaration of Independence. This paper helped the United States become its own country.

Abraham Lincoln was born in a log cabin in Kentucky in 1809. He later moved to Illinois. He taught himself how to read and study law. As president, he helped free African Americans from slavery.

Before Ronald Reagan became president he was an actor. He was born in Illinois in 1911. He became governor of California. As president he helped make peace with other countries.

Be a Sleuth

Look for Clues What information in the text could be used to write a biography of one of these presidents?

Ask Questions Write one question you still have about each of these presidents.

Make Your Case Use information from the text to tell how two of these presidents were similar and how two of them were different.

JOSH GIBSON, HOME RUN KING

Josh Gibson's first love was baseball. In his spare time, Gibson could be found improving his skills and showing off his talent. One night in 1930, Gibson went to watch his hometown team, the Homestead Grays, play against the Kansas City Monarchs. That night changed everything.

The Grays' catcher was injured. The team's owner remembered seeing eighteen-year-old Gibson play ball. He invited the young athlete to play that night. The owner was so impressed that he asked Gibson to join the team. Gibson played professional baseball for the rest of his life.

Josh Gibson was a great player. He hit hundreds of home runs. Gibson led the Negro National League in home runs for ten years. He could hit a baseball harder and farther than almost any other player in the history of the game. He was a skilled catcher too. He earned a place in the Baseball Hall of Fame. But Josh Gibson didn't play in the Major Leagues. The Major Leagues were closed to African American players at the time. Three months after Gibson's death in 1947, Jackie Robinson became the first African American to play in the Major Leagues. He carried on Gibson's tradition of baseball excellence.

BE A SLEUTH

Look for Clues What clues can you find that show baseball was important to Josh Gibson?

Ask Questions After reading the text, write three interesting questions related to baseball long ago.

Make Your Case What do you think are the four most important facts the writer shares about Josh Gibson?

Sleuth Tips

Look for Clues

How do sleuths remember clues?
- Sleuths don't expect to remember everything. They write down important details.
- Sleuths use many ways to remember clues. They might write a list or draw a picture.

Ask Questions

Why do sleuths ask questions?
- Sleuths ask questions to gather facts. These are often the easiest questions to answer.
- Sleuths also ask questions to make everyone think.

Make Your Case

How do sleuths work with other sleuths?
- Sleuths ask other people questions to find areas where everyone agrees.
- Sleuths want to hear ideas from others.

Prove It!

What do sleuths think about before showing what they have learned?
- Sleuths review what they have learned to decide what's important and what's not.
- Sleuths think about the best order to put things in before sharing them.

A Real-Life Action Hero

Eric listened closely to the first-aid lesson at his Cub Scout meeting. The guest speaker was talking about the Heimlich maneuver. This action can help someone who is choking. It causes whatever is caught in the choking person's throat to come out. Later Eric saw a television program that taught him more about it. He practiced with his mother. He followed the Cub Scout motto "Be prepared." He had no idea how important that lesson would be.

One day Eric's little sister Jessie was having a snack. Their mother heard Jessie choking. Jessie could not breathe. Nothing their mother did helped.

She called for Eric's help. Then she rushed to call 9-1-1. But Eric was ready. Before his mother could tell the 9-1-1 operator what was happening, Eric sprang into action. He wrapped his arms around Jessie from behind. He did exactly what he had practiced with his mother. The egg Jessie had been eating popped right out! Jessie was safely breathing again. Ten-year-old Eric was a hero.

Be a Sleuth

Look for Clues Why is the order of the events important in this selection? Use clues from the text in your answer.

Ask Questions After reading the text, what are two questions you have about what to do in a home emergency?

Make Your Case The writer tells about actual events. Do the fictional characters make the story more interesting or take away from the important information? Explain your answer.

The Blank Book

Elias's dad was in the army. He was leaving home to be stationed in another country. As he said good-bye, Dad gave Elias a book. "I want you to read this when you get home," Dad said.

Elias didn't feel like reading, but he opened the book anyway . . . and what a surprise! Every page was blank except the first one. There, Dad explained that they would take turns writing in the book, mailing it back and forth while Dad was gone.

Elias began writing immediately, telling his dad how much he missed him, and then he mailed the book. Three weeks later, the book came back. Dad wrote about a market he had visited. He described the sharp, spicy smells and bright, patterned carpets. He described the warm, buttery bread he tried.

Elias and his dad wrote often. Dad described what life was like on the base. Sometimes he invented silly stories or drew neat pictures. Elias wrote about home and school. He drew colorful pictures. They had to get another book before long, and then another!

When Dad came home, he had a new book with him. "I thought we could keep going," Dad said, grinning. Elias nodded. This was definitely a tradition he wanted to keep.

Be a Sleuth

Look for Clues Find clues that show how what Dad wrote in the book was similar to and different from what Elias wrote.

Ask Questions If you were Elias, what new questions might you want to ask Dad about where he was living?

Make Your Case If Elias and his dad are fictional characters, what parts of the story do you think are actual events?

CURTIS THE COWBOY COOK

Curtis was bored and unhappy. He thought when he was hired to work on the cattle drive that he'd finally get to be a real cowboy. But the cowboys treated him like a kid. The cook, Dusty, let Curtis help him. But Dusty was so busy he barely had time to talk. Curtis just watched and did chores for the cook all day long.

The chuckwagon always went ahead of the slow-moving cattle. That way, dinner would be ready when the cowboys got to camp each night. Dusty and Curtis started the cooking fire. As they carried water from a creek, Dusty slipped down the bank. He landed hard. Curtis helped Dusty limp painfully to camp. Then Curtis got to work with Dusty directing him.

He cut the salt pork and arranged it in deep pans. He scooped beans into the pans, covered them with water, and set them on the fire to boil. Soon the contents of the pans were bubbling, and the smell filled the camp. As the sun went down, the tired, hungry cowboys arrived. One bite of the hearty pork and beans was enough to convince them that Curtis was born to be a cowboy cook.

BE A SLEUTH

Look for Clues What clues can you find that show how the cowboys' feelings about Curtis change from the beginning to the end of the story?

Ask Questions After reading the text, what are two questions you have about cowboys and cattle drives?

Make Your Case The fictional characters in this story do things that real cowboys do. List the actual activities you find in the story.

Unit 5
Pioneering New Ideas and New Worlds

Hello, Sleuthhounds!

In this unit, you will be looking for clues about changes. Here are some sleuth tips to help you. Keep it up!

Sleuth Tips

Look for Clues
How do sleuths uncover clues from an author?
- Sleuths look for clues about sequence or how one event caused another.
- Sleuths work while they read. They try to make the clues fit together like a puzzle.

Ask Questions
Where do sleuths get answers to their questions?
- Sleuths find some answers in the words and pictures. They also talk to other sleuths.
- Sleuths look for answers in other books or on computers.

Make Your Case
How do sleuths use clues when they make a case?
- Sleuths tell what they think. They tell how the clues led them to their answer.
- Sleuths tell where they found the clues. This can be very useful.

Prove It!
Why do sleuths think about who will read what they write?
- Sleuths know that one type of writing doesn't work for every reader.
- Sleuths write in the form that is needed. Sometimes a sleuth writes a list. Sometimes a story or poem is what is needed.

Journey to FREEDOM

In 1854, William was an African American slave in North Carolina. He longed to be free, but that did not seem possible. Late one night, a friend woke up William. He wanted William to escape with him to Canada.

The thought of freedom made William joyful. But how would he and his friend get to Canada? It was hundreds of miles away. They had very little money or food. They had no maps. Where would they hide along the way? Soldiers and other people were looking everywhere for runaway slaves. The answer to his questions was the Underground Railroad.

The Underground Railroad was not a railroad. It was a network of people. The network helped enslaved people escape to freedom. Some "conductors" on the railroad led enslaved people by foot or wagon to safe places. Other people opened their homes and barns to give shelter. Some gave money, clothes, and food to help. Before the end of slavery in the United States, thousands of people used the Underground Railroad to escape slavery.

Even with all that help, the path to freedom was not easy. The trip often took weeks. It was very dangerous. Many of the people who used the railroad agreed that the long journey was a small price to pay for freedom.

Be a Sleuth

Look for Clues What words from the text help you understand how hard it was to escape from slavery?

Ask Questions After reading the text, what is one question you have about the Underground Railroad? Where could you learn more about it?

Make Your Case There are quotation marks around the word *conductor*. Why is this done? What does the word *conductor* mean in this selection?

A Journey North

Harlem is a very interesting place. In the early 1900s many African Americans headed north. They left the South to find a new life in the North. Many settled in Harlem. Harlem is a neighborhood in New York City.

Life in the South had been hard. There were few jobs. The North had more jobs and the chance of a better life.

African Americans hoped they would get jobs in factories in the North. They dreamt of making more money. They wanted better schools for their children.

Most African Americans lived in the South. Their journey north changed that. More than half of all African Americans moved from the South. However, some had never lived in cities. Cities were big and noisy. It was difficult to live in a new place. Many found comfort living in neighborhoods with other African Americans.

Harlem became the largest African American neighborhood in the country. A group of artists, musicians, and singers used their talents to show African American culture. Palmer Hayden painted paintings of African Americans in the South and the North. Other artists sang songs or wrote about their experiences. They shared the journeys of African Americans with America.

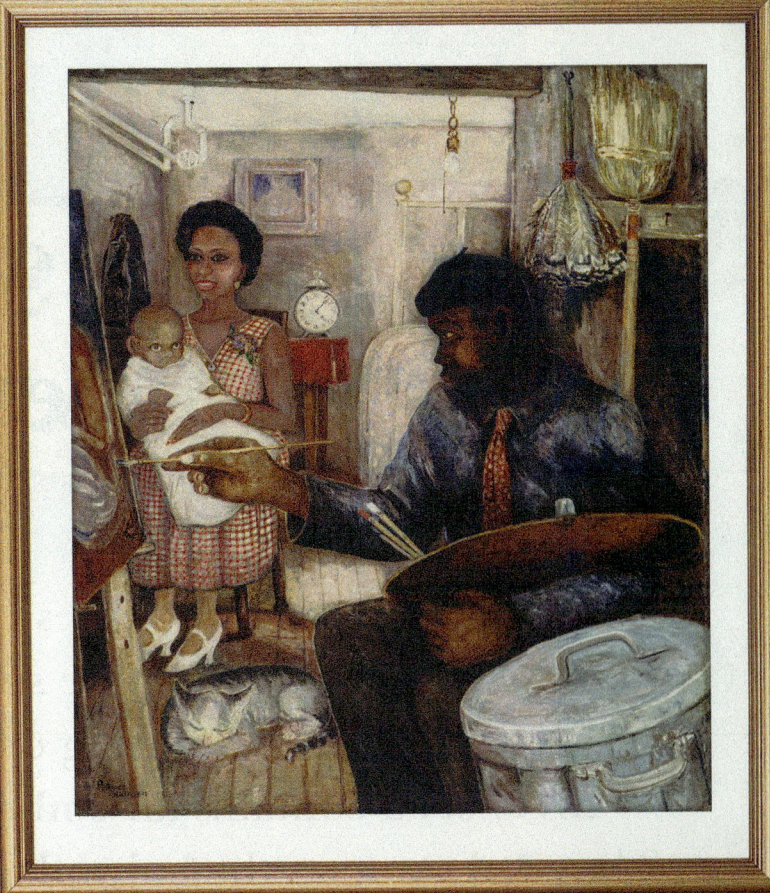

Be a Sleuth

Look for Clues Why does the writer think Harlem is interesting?

Ask Questions After reading, what are two questions you still have about Harlem?

Make Your Case Explain why people made the journey to Harlem. Use information from the text in your answer.

From Seed to Flower to Fruit

Do you know where apples come from? Have you ever seen an apple **seed?** Inside that tiny brown shell is the beginning of a whole new tree!

Every seed contains an **embryo,** or a baby plant. The seed protects the baby plant. Then when the seed gets the right amount of water and warmth, it breaks open. The embryo begins to grow.

A **stem** with little seed **leaves** pushes upward. There may be one leaf or two leaves. The **seedling** wants light to help it grow. **Roots** also begin to grow. They help the seedling get food from the soil.

New leaves grow from the stem. When there are enough new leaves, the seed leaves fall off. Soon **flower buds** appear. When the flowers open, bees move pollen from one **flower** to another. New seeds form inside the flowers. The part of the plant where these seeds are grows larger. It becomes a tiny **apple,** and soon it will be ready to eat. Do you see the seeds inside? Each seed is ready for a chance to become a new plant. The cycle begins again!

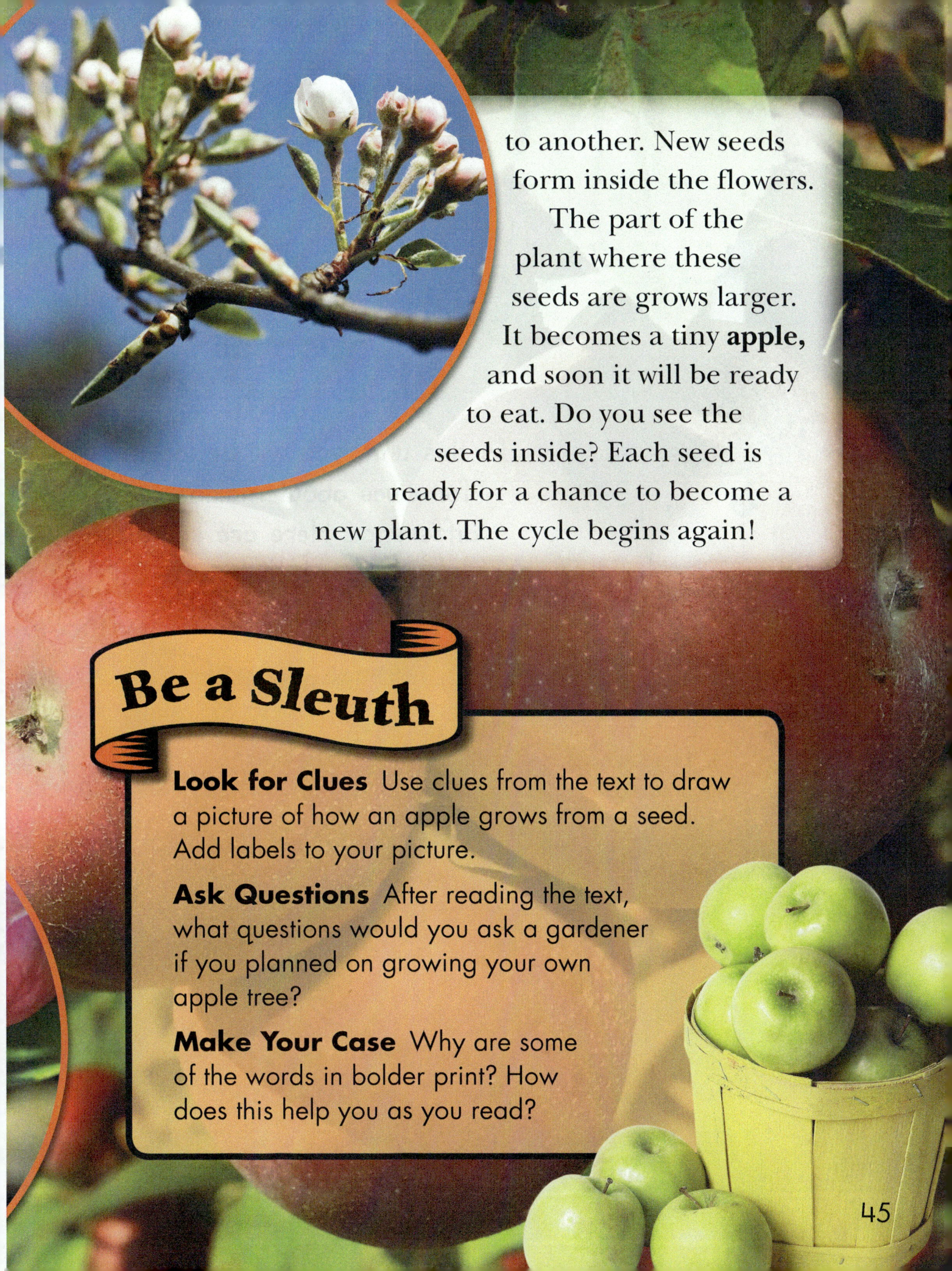

Be a Sleuth

Look for Clues Use clues from the text to draw a picture of how an apple grows from a seed. Add labels to your picture.

Ask Questions After reading the text, what questions would you ask a gardener if you planned on growing your own apple tree?

Make Your Case Why are some of the words in bolder print? How does this help you as you read?

Unit 6
Changing the World

Calling all Sleuthhounds!

In this unit, you will be looking for clues about making a difference. Here are some sleuth tips to help you. Here we go!

Sleuth Tips

Look for Clues

How do sleuths know if a clue is important?
- Sleuths find and record many clues. They don't always know which clues will be the important ones.
- Sleuths look for ways to fit the clues together.

Ask Questions

How do sleuths think of interesting questions to ask?
- Sleuths often ask for more information about a clue.
- Sleuths think about the questions that have not been answered.

Make Your Case

How do sleuths learn from other sleuths?
- Sleuths listen to others. What clues did they find?
- Sleuths ask questions to understand what others are thinking.

Prove It!

How do sleuths prepare to share what they know?
- Sleuths know that most things aren't perfect on the first try. They reread and rewrite to make it better.
- Sleuths get better with practice. Practice makes sharing easier and more fun.

Picking Up Sunset Park

Lacey stood at the gate of Sunset Park. What she saw made her want to cry. The storm had knocked down two small trees and scattered branches everywhere.

Her brother, Jared, looked at the mess. "We might as well go home," he said. "It's going to be a while before we can play here again."

"Let's pick up some of the branches," Lacey said.

"That will take all day!" Jared said.

"If we work together, we can get it done quickly," Lacey said.

They began to pick up branches and pile them near the gate. As the pile grew, their friends Marius and Elsa rode by.

"What's going on?" Marius asked.

"The storm blew down some trees," Lacey said. "We're cleaning up."

Marius and Elsa hopped off their bikes and began working. Soon, some neighbors saw the kids at work. They started to help clean up too. Mrs. Cleary came with cold lemonade for everyone. Before long, the branches were all cleared. The adults cut the fallen trees and moved them to the side. The park was almost as good as new. Lacey and Jared happily ran to the swings. They were thrilled. There was even time to play before dinner!

Be a Sleuth

Look for Clues What clues in the story tell you how bad the storm damage was?

Ask Questions What are two questions you would ask one of the neighbors who stopped to help?

Make Your Case What did the writer want to explain in this story? How do you know?

Making a Difference, ONE BAG at a TIME

Annie Wignall founded Care Bags Foundation.

When Annie Wignall was eleven, her mother told her something that made her sad. She said that some children have to leave their homes in hard times. They often must leave everything behind. They lose many things that they love and need. Annie wanted to do something to help.

Annie made cute cloth bags for children in need. She found people to donate new items that children might miss from their homes. Annie filled the bags with these things. She put in soap and toothpaste. She found toys to add. She got games and books for the bags. She hoped to give these children lots to make them happy.

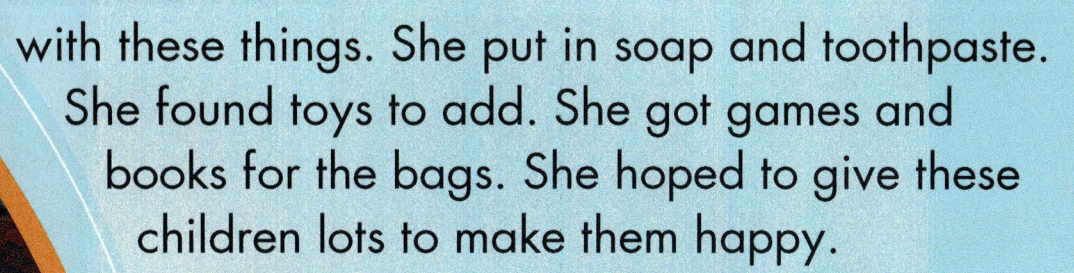

Annie started Care Bags Foundation. Every month Annie and other helpers prepare about one hundred Care Bags 4 Kids. Some people sew the bags. Others give things to put in the bags. Volunteers help fill them. The bags are then given to children in need. They bring many smiles!

Care Bags Foundation also helps children in another way. It teaches kids how to make a difference. It tells how to start a Care Bags project in their own towns. Care Bags Foundation has made a big difference with each small bag!

Be a Sleuth

Look for Clues What are two events in the text that caused something else to happen?

Ask Questions What are two questions you would ask Annie Wignall to find out more about Care Bags Foundation?

Make Your Case The writer writes that the Care Bags Foundation makes a big difference. What support does the writer provide?

WANTED: Great Student Leaders!

Do you have lots of school spirit and fun ideas for helping your school? Are you a good leader? Then you may belong on the student council!

Many schools have student councils. These are groups of students who are chosen to share ideas and make decisions about student activities. Students often elect student council members in a class or grade-level election. Council members work hard to be good students, good citizens, and good examples to everyone at school.

Some students are officers with special duties. They lead the council meetings, keep records, and work with school staff members. Others are representatives. They talk to the students in their classes to get ideas. Later, they report back to the class about decisions the student council has made.

But what does a student council actually *do?* It might organize an event, such as a school carnival. It might raise money for new equipment. It might plan volunteer activities, such as a food drive, to help people in the community. If there is a problem in the school, the student council may discuss possible solutions to the problem.

Are you ready to make a difference in your school? If so, the student council may be the place for you!

Be a Sleuth

Look for Clues What are some clues that you find in the pictures and text that help you better understand what a student council does?

Ask Questions After reading the text, what would you ask students on a student council?

Make Your Case What do you think the text trying to describe in this selection? List words that help with the description.

DONATION BOX

Acknowledgments

Photographs

Every effort has been made to secure permission and provide appropriate credit for photographic material. The publisher deeply regrets any omission and pledges to correct errors called to its attention in subsequent editions.

Unless otherwise acknowledged, all photographs are the property of Pearson Education, Inc.

Photo locators denoted as follows: Top (T), Center (C), Bottom (B), Left (L), Right (R), Background (Bkgd)

Cover Chandler Digital Art

4 (Bkgd) Nightman/Fotolia,(TL) kontur-vid/Fotolia,(C) Kev Llewellyn /Shutterstock,(TR) Zedcor Wholly Owned/Thinkstock; **5** (Bkgd) Warakorn/Fotolia; (TR) Hemera Technologies/Thinkstock,(CR) PaulPaladin/Fotolia,(BR) rrrob/Fotolia; **8** Shane Trotter/Shutterstock; **9** (CL) Jupiterimages/Thinkstock,(BR) uwimages/Fotolia; **10** Elenathewise/Fotolia; **11** Pearson Education; **12** Alexei Novikov/Fotolia; **13** Digital Vision/Thinkstock; **16** (CL) Olga Sapegina/Fotolia,(BR) Comstock/Thinkstock; **17** Oleksandr Moroz/Fotolia; **18** (TL) Aleksandr Vasilyev/Fotolia, (BR) Creatas/Thinkstock, (Border) Aptyp-koK/Fotolia, (C) Andres Rodriguez/Fotolia,(BR) Philippe Devanne/Fotolia; **20** (TL) Sharpshot/Fotolia, (CL) Glenda Powers/Fotolia, (B) Kredo/Fotolia,(BR) Gudellaphoto/Fotolia; **21** (TL) sax/Fotolia, (CL) Laurent Renault/Fotolia,(C) Jupiterimages/Thinkstock; **24** (CR) Mary Evans Picture Library/Alamy, (Bkgd) Tom Brakefield/Thinkstock; **25** (TR) tanya18/Fotolia, (BL) Photos.com/Thinkstock; **26** (Bkgd) Vege/Fotolia; (T) Library of Congress, (CR) Steve Wood/Shutterstock; **27** (TR) Library of Congress, (CR) Pearson Education,(CL) Pearson Education, (BR) Pearson Education; **28** (Bkgd) Jim Mills/Fotolia; **32** (Bkgd) Kit Wai Chan/Fotolia, (C) Pearson Education; **33** Stockbyte/Thinkstock; **34** (Bkgd) Javarman/Fotolia,(BL) Gaelj/Fotolia,(BC) Douglas Freer/Fotolia,(C) Barbara Helgason/Fotolia; **35** (Bkgd) Luminas/Fotolia,(TR) Thinkstock,(BR) Victor B/Fotolia, (Bkgd) Comstock/Thinkstock, (BR) Kevin Largent/Fotolia; **37** TR Jupiterimages/Fotolia; **37** (BL) Sarunya_foto/Fotolia; **40** (Bkgd) lacabetyar/Fotolia,(BR) iMagine/Fotolia, (C) Mates/Fotolia,(C) David M Schrader/Fotolia; **41** Thinkstock; **42** (Bkgd) Hemera Technologies/Thinkstock,(CC) Klavlav/Fotolia; **42** (C) zagart117/Fotolia, (T) Hemera Technologies/Thinkstock; **43** (BR) Rusian Olinchuk/Fotolia; **44** (TL) James Stevenson/Dorling Kindersley Ltd, (TC) Dynamic Graphics/Thinkstock, (CR) Geoff Dann/Dorling Kindersley Ltd; **44** (Bkgd) Justimagine/Fotolia, (BR) Jenny Thompson/Fotolia; **45** (TR) Unpict/Fotolia, (BR) Hemera Technologies/Thinkstock; **48** (T) picsfive/Fotolia, (C) photka/Fotolia,(Bkgd) Melinda Fawver/Shutterstock; **49** Stockbyte/Thinkstock; **50** Care Bags Foundation; **52** Monkey Business/Fotolia; **53** mangostock/Fotolia.